Hanukkah

By ALLAN MOREY

Illustrations by LUKE SÉGUIN-MAGEE

Music by MARK OBLINGER

CANTATA
LEARNING

WWW.CANTATALEARNING.COM

CANTATA LEARNING

Published by Cantata Learning
1710 Roe Crest Drive
North Mankato, MN 56003
www.cantatalearning.com

Library of Congress Cataloging-in-Publication Data
Names: Morey, Allan, author. | Séguin Magee, Luke, illustrator. | Oblinger,
    Mark, composer.
Title: Hanukkah : by Allan Morey ; illustrations by Luke Séguin-Magee ;
    music by Mark Oblinger.
Description: North Mankato, MN : Cantata Learning, [2017] | Series: Holidays
    in rhythm and rhyme | Age: 5-8 ; Grade K-3.
Identifiers: LCCN 2017007564 (print) | LCCN 2017009550 (ebook) | ISBN
    9781684100330 (hardcover : alk. paper) | ISBN 9781684100347
Subjects: LCSH: Hanukkah--Juvenile literature. | Hanukkah--Songs and music.
Classification: LCC BM695.H3 M67 2017 (print) | LCC BM695.H3 (ebook) | DDC
    296.4/35--dc23
LC record available at https://lccn.loc.gov/201700756

Book design, Tim Palin Creative
Editorial direction, Flat Sole Studio
Executive musical production and direction, Elizabeth Draper
Music arranged and produced by Mark Oblinger

Printed in the United States of America in North Mankato, Minnesota.
072017   0367CGF17

ACCESS THE MUSIC!

SCAN CODE WITH MOBILE APP

CANTATALEARNING.COM

TIPS TO SUPPORT LITERACY AT HOME

WHY READING AND SINGING WITH YOUR CHILD IS SO IMPORTANT

Daily reading with your child leads to increased academic achievement. Music and songs, specifically rhyming songs, are a fun and easy way to build early literacy and language development. Music skills correlate significantly with both phonological awareness and reading development. Singing helps build vocabulary and speech development. And reading and appreciating music together is a wonderful way to strengthen your relationship.

READ AND SING EVERY DAY!

TIPS FOR USING CANTATA LEARNING BOOKS AND SONGS DURING YOUR DAILY STORY TIME

1. As you sing and read, point out the different words on the page that rhyme. Suggest other words that rhyme.

2. Memorize simple rhymes such as Itsy Bitsy Spider and sing them together. This encourages comprehension skills and early literacy skills.

3. Use the questions in the back of each book to guide your singing and storytelling.

4. Read the included sheet music with your child while you listen to the song. How do the music notes correlate to the words of the song?

5. Sing along on the go and at home. Access music by scanning the QR code on each Cantata book. You can also stream or download the music for free to your computer, smartphone, or mobile device.

Devoting time to daily reading shows that you are available for your child. Together, you are building language, literacy, and listening skills.

Have fun reading and singing!

Hanukkah begins in December and lasts eight days. It is also known as the **Festival** of Lights. Long ago, the Jewish people fought for the right to worship their religion. After freeing one of their temples, a priest noticed there was only enough oil to keep the temple lamp burning for one night. But miraculously, the lamp kept burning for eight days!

To learn why Hanukkah is such a special holiday, turn the page and sing along!

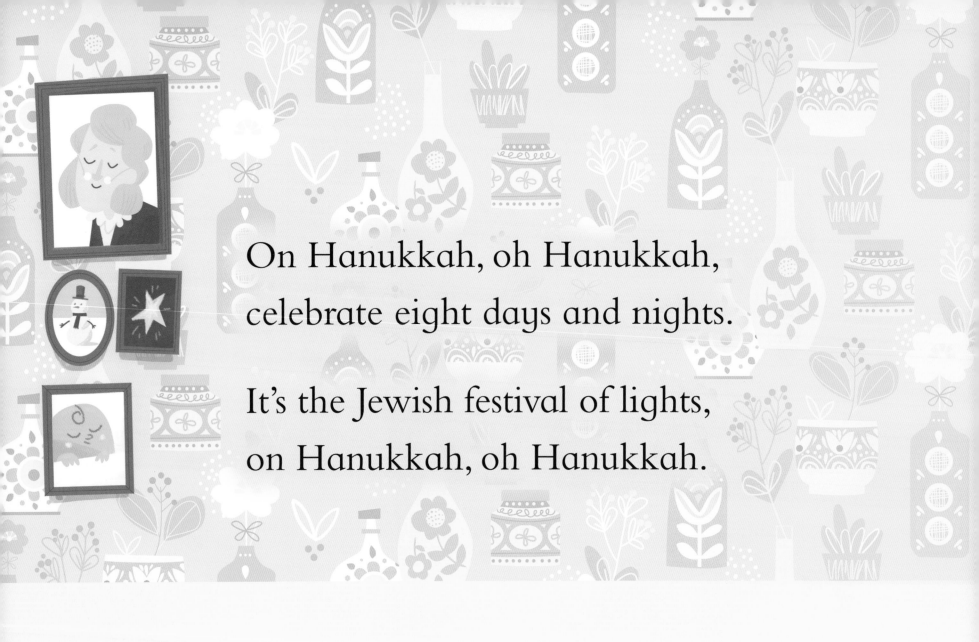

On Hanukkah, oh Hanukkah,
celebrate eight days and nights.

It's the Jewish festival of lights,
on Hanukkah, oh Hanukkah.

On Hanukkah, oh Hanukkah,
put a candle in the menorah.

Put a candle in the menorah
on Hanukkah, oh Hanukkah.

On Hanukkah, oh Hanukkah,
in the window there's a menorah.

The candles are all **aglow**
on Hanukkah, oh Hanukkah.

On Hanukkah, oh Hanukkah,
put a candle in the menorah.

Put a candle in the menorah
on Hanukkah, oh Hanukkah.

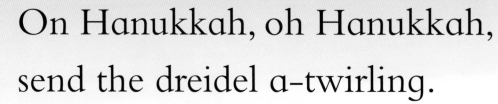

On Hanukkah, oh Hanukkah,
send the dreidel a-twirling.

Send the dreidel a-whirling
on Hanukkah, oh Hanukkah.

On Hanukkah, oh Hanukkah,
eat **latkes** and other treats.

Sing songs with family, oh, so sweet
on Hanukkah, oh Hanukkah.

On Hanukkah, oh Hanukkah,
you receive **gelt** from your parents.

Get candy and get presents
on Hanukkah, oh Hanukkah.

On Hanukkah, oh Hanukkah,
celebrate eight days and nights.

It's the Jewish festival of lights,
on Hanukkah, oh Hanukkah.

It's the Jewish festival of lights,
on Hanukkah, oh Hanukkah.

SONG LYRICS
Hanukkah

On Hanukkah, oh Hanukkah,
celebrate eight days and nights.
It's the Jewish festival of lights,
on Hanukkah, oh Hanukkah.

On Hanukkah, oh Hanukkah,
put a candle in the menorah.
Put a candle in the menorah
on Hanukkah, oh Hanukkah.

On Hanukkah, oh Hanukkah,
in the window, there's a menorah
The candles are all aglow
on Hanukkah, oh Hanukkah.

On Hanukkah, oh Hanukkah,
put a candle in the menorah.
Put a candle in the menorah
on Hanukkah, oh Hanukkah.

On Hanukkah, oh Hanukkah,
send the dreidel a-twirling.
Send the dreidel a-whirling
on Hanukkah, oh Hanukkah.

On Hanukkah, oh Hanukkah,
eat latkes and other treats.
Sing songs with family, oh, so sweet
on Hanukkah, oh Hanukkah.

On Hanukkah, oh Hanukkah,
you receive gelt from your parents.
Get candy and get presents
on Hanukkah, oh Hanukkah.

On Hanukkah, oh Hanukkah,
celebrate eight days and nights.
It's the Jewish festival of lights,
on Hanukkah, oh Hanukkah.

It's the Jewish festival of lights,
on Hanukkah, oh Hanukkah.

Hanukkah

Holiday
Mark Oblinger

Intro/Outro

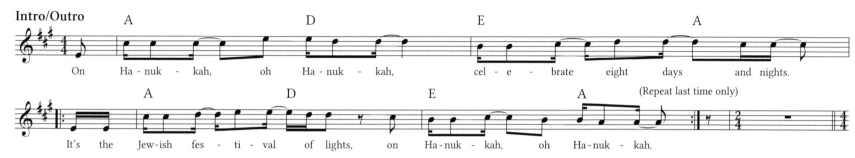

On Ha-nuk-kah, oh Ha-nuk-kah, cel-e-brate eight days and nights.

(Repeat last time only)

It's the Jew-ish fes-ti-val of lights, on Ha-nuk-kah, oh Ha-nuk-kah.

Interlude

Verse

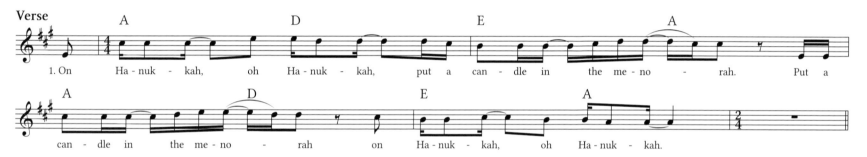

1. On Ha-nuk-kah, oh Ha-nuk-kah, put a can-dle in the me-no-rah. Put a

can-dle in the me-no-rah on Ha-nuk-kah, oh Ha-nuk-kah.

Verse 2
On Hanukkah, oh Hanukkah,
in the window, there's a menorah
The candles are all aglow
on Hanukkah, oh Hanukkah.

Interlude

Verse 3
On Hanukkah, oh Hanukkah,
put a candle in the menorah.
Put a candle in the menorah
on Hanukkah, oh Hanukkah.

Interlude

Verse 4
On Hanukkah, oh Hanukkah,
send the dreidel a-twirling.
Send the dreidel a-whirling
on Hanukkah, oh Hanukkah.

Interlude

Verse 5
On Hanukkah, oh Hanukkah,
eat latkes and other treats.
Sing songs with family, oh, so sweet
on Hanukkah, oh Hanukkah.

Interlude

Verse 6
On Hanukkah, oh Hanukkah,
you receive gelt from your parents.
Get candy and get presents
on Hanukkah, oh Hanukkah.

Interlude

Outro

Interlude

GLOSSARY

aglow—giving off a steady, low light

festival—a celebration or holiday

gelt—money or sometimes chocolate coins wrapped in gold foil

latkes—potato pancakes

GUIDED READING ACTIVITIES

1. In this book, you see people lighting candles in a menorah. Draw a menorah of your own. How many candles will you put in it? Remember, the middle candle is always lit.

2. On Hanukkah, people play a game by spinning a dreidel. What type of games do you like to play with your family and friends?

3. People celebrate Hanukkah by eating special foods and giving presents. Can you think of any other holidays that people celebrate by having family feasts or giving gifts? What foods do they eat? What do they give each other?

TO LEARN MORE

Dickmann, Nancy. *Hanukkah*. Chicago: Heinemann Library, 2011.

Felix, Rebecca. *We Celebrate Hanukkah in Winter*. Ann Arbor, MI: Cherry Lake, 2015.

Pettiford, Rebecca. *Hanukkah*. Minneapolis: Jump!, 2014.

Randall, Ronne. *Hanukkah* Sweets and Treats. New York: Windmill Books, 2013.